The Woman of Enneagram 6: Love, Marriage, Success Edition

Enneagram For Women, Volume 6

Maria Rondon

Published by Maria Rondon, 2024.

MARIA RONDON
THE WOMAN OF
ENNEAGRAM
6

LOVE, MARRIAGE AND SUCCESS EDITION

While every precaution has been taken in the preparation of this book, the publisher assumes no responsibility for errors or omissions, or for damages resulting from the use of the information contained herein.

THE WOMAN OF ENNEAGRAM 6: LOVE, MARRIAGE, SUCCESS EDITION

First edition. March 28, 2024.

Copyright © 2024 Maria Rondon.

ISBN: 979-8227418241

Written by Maria Rondon.

CONTENT

Enneagram for Type 6 Women: The Loyal Guardian

Chapter 1: The Enneagram and You: A Compass for Self-Discovery

- A brief historical overview of the Enneagram and its relevance to female self-awareness.
- The importance of self-awareness for women: exploring how self-understanding benefits Type 6 women in different areas of their lives.

Chapter 2: The Type 6 Woman: The Loyal Guardian in Her Essence

- Delving into the core characteristics, motivations, fears, and desires of the Type 6 woman.
- The two instinctual variants (self-preservation and social) and their influence on the personality of the Type 6 woman.

Chapter 3: Navigating Relationships with the Enneagram

- How the Enneagram helps you understand type differences and strengthen relationships.

Chapter 4: Building Trust and Security: The Foundation of Strong Relationships

- The importance of trust and security for Type 6 women in their relationships.
- Strategies for fostering effective communication and strengthening relationships with partners, friends, and family.

Chapter 5: Meet Your Tribe: Building Support Networks

- The value of strong friendships and social support for the Type 6 woman.
- Tips for building and maintaining strong relationships with friends and colleagues.

Chapter 6: Discovering Your Purpose: Career and Vocation

- Identifying your strengths and passions to find a meaningful career.
- Strategies for overcoming indecision and fear of failure in the workplace.

Chapter 7: Cultivating Inner Strength: Resilience and Self-Compassion

- Developing resilience to face challenges and self-criticism.
- Techniques for managing anxiety and cultivating self-compassion.

Chapter 8: Holistic Well-being: Body and Mind in Balance

- The importance of mindful nutrition for the physical and emotional health of the Type 6 woman.
- The role of physical exercise in stress management and overall well-being

Chapter 9: The Enneagram and Spirituality: Deepening Your Connection

- How the Enneagram can be a tool for deepening the spiritual connection of the Type 6 woman.
- Exploring various spiritual practices that resonate with Type 6 women.

Chapter 10: Your Wings: Unfolding Your Complexity

- Description of the wings (Type 6w5 and Type 6w7) and their influence on the personality, strengths, and challenges of the Type 6 woman.

Chapter 11: Integration and Disintegration: On the Path of Evolution

- Understanding the integration process towards Type 9 and disintegration towards Type 3 of the Type 6 woman.

Chapter 1:

The Enneagram and You: A Compass for Self-Discovery

The chapter, "The Enneagram and You: A Compass for Self-Discovery," seeks to explore the Enneagram's historical significance and its profound relevance to female self-awareness. This ancient typology system, veiled in the annals of history, offers not just a map for understanding the diverse personalities that color our world but also serves as a mirror reflecting the intricate tapestry of the female psyche.

Tracing the Enneagram's roots, we delve into a past where geometry and spirituality intertwined, pointing to a truth beyond the visible. Its beginnings, shrouded in the mists of time, whisper of a synthesis of wisdom from the mystical Sufi traditions, the sacred geometry of the Pythagoreans, and the spiritual insights of the Desert Fathers. This confluence of knowledge from various cultures and epochs underscores the Enneagram's universal appeal and its timeless quest to decode the human spirit.

The transformation of the Enneagram from an esoteric symbol to a tool for deep psychological insight is a testament to the human yearning for self-understanding. George Gurdjieff, a figure pivotal to the Enneagram's modern journey, unveiled it as a window into the soul's dynamics, emphasizing the importance of self-observation and inner work. His teachings, though complex, laid the groundwork for subsequent explorations into the Enneagram's application in personal growth and development.

As the Enneagram's teachings permeated the West, it encountered a burgeoning feminist movement, ripe for a framework that could articulate the unique challenges and strengths of women's experiences. The system's flexibility and depth offer a unique lens through which to view female identity, not as a monolith but as a spectrum of archetypes, each with its own story and path to empowerment.

For women, the Enneagram provides a language to articulate their inner experiences, a navigational tool for the journey of self-discovery. It invites a dialogue with the self, encouraging introspection and the uncovering of layers that define personal identity. In understanding their

Enneagram type, women can embark on a path of self-acceptance, recognizing their strengths and confronting their vulnerabilities with compassion and courage.

This journey is particularly resonant in a world that often seeks to define women by external standards. The Enneagram empowers women to define themselves on their own terms, to embrace their complexities, and to forge a path of personal growth that is both authentic and transformative. It challenges societal norms, urging a reexamination of what it means to be strong, nurturing, assertive, or emotional, and highlights the unique contributions of each type to the collective tapestry of human experience.

In the context of female self-awareness, the Enneagram transcends its historical origins to become a beacon of empowerment and enlightenment. It does not offer easy answers but rather, poses profound questions that prompt a deeper engagement with the self and the world. Through the lens of the Enneagram, women can explore the multifaceted nature of their identity, embracing the full spectrum of their humanity with wisdom and grace.

Thus, the Enneagram stands not just as a testament to the rich tapestry of human knowledge and spirituality but as a living, evolving guide to understanding the depths of the female soul. In the ongoing dance of self-discovery, it offers a compass to navigate the complex, often tumultuous waters of life, enabling women to chart a course toward authentic self-expression and fulfillment.

"The Importance of Self-Awareness for Women

Exploring How Self-Understanding Benefits Type 6 Women in Different Areas of Their Lives," aims to unravel the threads of introspection and self-discovery, showcasing how they weave into the fabric of a Type 6 woman's existence, enriching her relationships, career, and personal growth.

Self-awareness, the bedrock of emotional intelligence, serves as a beacon, guiding Type 6 women through the often tumultuous sea of doubts and fears that mark their journey. Known as "The Loyalist," Type 6 women are characterized by their reliability, warmth, and profound sense of responsibility. However, these commendable traits are frequently shadowed by their internal struggles with anxiety and skepticism. It is here, in the heart of their uncertainties, that self-awareness lights the path toward tranquility and assurance.

In the realm of relationships, self-awareness empowers Type 6 women to navigate their intrinsic need for security and trust. By understanding their deep-seated fears of abandonment and betrayal, they can engage in open, honest dialogues with their partners, fostering a foundation built on mutual respect and understanding. This introspective journey encourages Type 6 women to confront their vulnerabilities, allowing them to forge connections that are not only supportive but also deeply enriching.

Turning to the professional landscape, self-awareness acts as a compass, guiding Type 6 women toward realizing their potential while managing their anxieties. The workplace, often a source of stress for Type 6s, becomes a stage for demonstrating their remarkable problem-solving skills and loyalty. Recognizing their tendency to foresee problems can be a double-edged sword, self-awareness enables them to strike a balance between caution and decisiveness. By channeling their concern into constructive preparation and teamwork, they emerge as invaluable assets, leaders who navigate challenges with foresight and empathy.

Furthermore, self-awareness illuminates the path to personal growth for Type 6 women, inviting them to embrace their strengths while acknowledging their fears. This internal exploration fosters resilience, teaching them that vulnerability is not a weakness but a gateway to courage and transformation. As they learn to trust in their inner compass, the journey of self-discovery emboldens Type 6 women to step out of their comfort zones, embracing change with an open heart and a steadfast spirit.

In this quest for self-awareness, the Enneagram serves as a mirror, reflecting the complex interplay of traits that define Type 6 women. It challenges them to question, to delve deeper into the why behind their actions and thoughts. This reflective practice not only enhances their understanding of themselves but also enriches their interactions with the world around them.

The narrative of self-awareness for Type 6 women is thus a testament to the transformative power of introspection. It is a journey marked by moments of vulnerability, strength, and profound insight. In the grand tapestry of life, self-awareness is the thread that binds, a guiding light that leads to a fuller, more authentic existence. Through the lens of the Enneagram, Type 6 women are invited to embark on this journey, a pilgrimage of the soul that promises not just self-discovery but a deeper connection to the essence of who they truly are.

Chapter 2:

The Type 6 Woman: The Loyal Guardian in Her Essence

This chapter aims to dissect and understand the core characteristics, motivations, fears, and desires that define the Type 6 woman, thereby providing a compass for those who identify with this type to navigate their inner landscapes with greater clarity and depth.

At the core of the Type 6 personality lies a paradox of strength and vulnerability, a testament to the complex nature of the human spirit. Known as The Loyal Guardian, the Type 6 woman is a bastion of reliability, commitment, and warmth. Her essence is characterized by an unwavering sense of duty and a profound capacity for empathy, making her a pillar of support for those she holds dear. However, these laudable traits are often underpinned by a continuous undercurrent of anxiety and a pervasive sense of insecurity.

Motivation for the Type 6 woman springs from a deep-seated desire for stability and security. This is not merely a quest for physical safety but an emotional and psychological sanctuary where doubts are quieted, and trust prevails. In her world, predictability is a balm to the tumultuous seas of uncertainty that often swirl within her. Thus, she is driven by the need to forge strong, dependable relationships and to create environments that are both harmonious and steadfast.

Yet, this quest for security is invariably intertwined with the Type 6 woman's fears. At her core, she grapples with anxieties concerning abandonment and betrayal. The thought of losing the trust and support of those she values can be paralyzing, leading to a vigilance that sometimes borders on suspicion. This internal struggle often manifests in a tendency towards skepticism, where the Type 6 woman may question the intentions of others, always preparing for unforeseen dangers that might never materialize.

Despite these challenges, the desires of the Type 6 woman reflect her profound yearning for peace and assurance. She seeks to build a life that is not only secure but also meaningful. Her loyalty, once given, is unwavering, and she dreams of reciprocal bonds where trust is both absolute and mutual. In her ideal world, fears are faced with courage, and vulnerabilities are shared without judgment, creating a foundation of unshakeable trust and understanding.

Understanding the Type 6 woman requires delving into these dimensions of her personality, recognizing the interplay between her strengths and vulnerabilities. It is a journey into acknowledging how her fears shape her motivations and how her desires for security and stability influence her relationships and worldview.

In embracing her essence, the Type 6 woman learns that her anxieties, while a significant part of her, do not define her entirety. Through self-awareness and growth, she discovers the strength to trust in her resilience and the courage to embrace uncertainty with an open heart. This process of self-discovery not only enriches her own life but also strengthens the bonds she forms with others, making her a true guardian of the connections that give life its depth and meaning.

Thus, "The Type 6 Woman: The Loyal Guardian in Her Essence" is not just a narrative of fears and challenges but a celebration of the Type 6 woman's capacity for loyalty, empathy, and strength. It is an invitation to explore the depths of her personality, to understand the nuances that make her who she is, and to acknowledge the beauty in her complexity. Through this journey, the Type 6 woman learns to navigate her inner world with grace, transforming her vulnerabilities into sources of power and her fears into stepping stones towards a richer, more fulfilled existence.

Self-Preservation Instinct in Type 6 Women

The self-preservation variant within Type 6 women accentuates their inherent desire for safety and security. This instinct amplifies their concern for physical well-being, not just for themselves but also for those they care about. It manifests in a keen awareness of their environment, an acute sense of vigilance, and a penchant for preparing against potential hazards. The self-preservation Type 6 woman is the epitome of prudence and foresight, often anticipating problems before they arise and crafting contingency plans to safeguard against them.

However, this heightened sense of caution can also lead to increased anxiety and stress, as the world is perceived through a lens of potential threats and uncertainties. These women may struggle with a pervasive sense of insecurity, constantly seeking stable ground in an ever-changing landscape. Their quest for self-preservation compels them to create a sanctuary that is both a physical and emotional stronghold, a place where the unpredictabilities of life can be managed and mitigated.

Social Instinct in Type 6 Women

On the other hand, the social variant of the Type 6 woman places a stronger emphasis on belonging and community. These individuals are deeply attuned to the dynamics of their social environment, valuing the strength found in unity and cooperation. The social Type 6 woman is inherently aware of her role within the group, often acting as the glue that holds relationships together. She is a loyal friend, a committed colleague, and a stabilizing presence in any social setting.

Yet, this external focus brings its own set of challenges. Social Type 6 women may experience anxiety related to their standing within the group, fearing rejection or abandonment. They are acutely sensitive to shifts in social harmony and can become preoccupied with maintaining alliances and preventing conflict. Their desire for social security drives them to seek affirmation and reassurance from others, sometimes at the expense of their inner peace.

The Interplay of Instincts in the Type 6 Personality

The interplay between the self-preservation and social instincts in Type 6 women creates a rich tapestry of behaviors and motivations. While both variants share a common thread of seeking security, the means and focus of their pursuit diverge, painting a multifaceted picture of the Type 6 personality.

For the self-preservation Type 6, security is found in tangible measures—financial stability, health, and a safe home environment. For the social Type 6, security is sought in intangible forms—relationships, social networks, and the feeling of being valued within a community. Regardless of the dominant instinct, both variants navigate the world with caution, guided by a deep-seated desire to find stability in an unpredictable world.

Understanding the influence of these instinctual variants is crucial for Type 6 women as they embark on their journey of self-discovery. By recognizing the underlying motivations and fears that drive their actions, they can begin to address their anxieties in a more constructive manner. This awareness enables them to strike a balance between seeking security and embracing the uncertainties of life, fostering a sense of inner peace and resilience.

Thus, the exploration of the self-preservation and social instincts within the Type 6 woman not only illuminates the nuances of her personality but also offers a pathway to greater self-understanding and growth. It reveals how the instinctual variants shape her interactions with the world, influencing her relationships, career choices, and personal development. Through this lens, the Type 6 woman can navigate her fears with courage and cultivate a life that reflects her true essence, grounded in the strength of her loyalty and the depth of her guardian spirit.

Chapter 3:
Navigating Relationships with the Enneagram

The Enneagram, as a system steeped in ancient wisdom and psychological insight, offers more than just a classification of personality types. It provides a nuanced framework for understanding the underlying motivations, fears, and desires that drive human behavior. For Type 6 women, known for their loyalty, caution, and sometimes anxiety, the Enneagram serves as a guide in deciphering the complex web of human emotions and interactions. It teaches that each personality type brings its own perspective, strengths, and challenges to relationships, highlighting the importance of empathy, communication, and mutual respect.

Understanding Type Differences

At the heart of the Enneagram's contribution to relationship dynamics is its ability to shed light on the profound differences in how individuals perceive the world and interact with others. For a Type 6 woman, this insight can be revolutionary. It helps her recognize that what she perceives as caution might be seen as indecision by a Type 7, known for their spontaneity and adventurous spirit, or that her need for reassurance might overwhelm a Type 5, who values independence and privacy.

This awareness fosters a greater understanding of the inevitable conflicts and misunderstandings that arise in relationships. Instead of attributing these to personal failings or incompatibility, the Enneagram encourages a deeper exploration of each type's intrinsic nature. It offers a language to articulate differences and a framework for navigating them, transforming potential sources of conflict into opportunities for growth.

Strengthening Relationships

The true power of the Enneagram in relationships lies in its capacity to inspire growth, compassion, and a deeper connection between individuals. By encouraging a journey inward, it equips Type 6 women with the self-awareness needed to approach relationships with openness and authenticity. This self-understanding becomes the foundation for building trust and understanding with others, allowing for more meaningful and fulfilling interactions.

For instance, a Type 6 woman's knowledge of her own tendencies towards anxiety and doubt can help her communicate her needs more clearly, reducing misunderstandings and fostering a supportive environment. Similarly, understanding a partner's or friend's core motivations and fears can lead to a more compassionate and empathetic approach to conflicts and challenges.

Moreover, the Enneagram encourages the cultivation of virtues that counterbalance the limitations of each type. For a Type 6, this might mean developing courage to confront fears, or for a Type 3, focusing on authenticity over achievement. These virtues not only contribute to personal growth but also enrich relationships, as individuals learn to bring out the best in each other.

In essence, the Enneagram does not offer a one-size-fits-all solution to relationship challenges. Instead, it provides a map for navigating the complex terrain of human connections, celebrating the diversity of personalities and the unique contributions of each type. For Type 6 women, and indeed for individuals of all types, the Enneagram becomes a compass for fostering deeper, more resilient relationships. It invites us to understand and appreciate the myriad ways in which people relate to the world and to each other, paving the way for connections that are rooted in mutual respect, understanding, and love.

Thus, "Navigating Relationships with the Enneagram" is not merely a chapter in a book; it is an invitation to embark on a journey of self-discovery and connection. It challenges us to look beyond the surface, to embrace the complexity of human nature, and to cultivate relationships that are not just enduring but transformative. Through the wisdom of the Enneagram, we learn that the key to stronger relationships lies in our ability to understand, accept, and celebrate the differences that make each of us uniquely ourselves.

Chapter 4:

Building Trust and Security: The Foundation of Strong Relationships

The Importance of Trust and Security for Type 6 Women in Their Relationships

In the labyrinth of human connections, the quest for trust and security forms the bedrock upon which Type 6 women build the edifice of their relationships. Just as the Enneagram traces its enigmatic roots back through the corridors of time, intertwining with the spiritual, philosophical, and psychological tapestry of human history, the narrative of Type 6 women weaves its threads through the intricate dance of trust and doubt, security and vulnerability.

For Type 6 women, relationships are not mere transient interactions but profound bonds that offer a sanctuary from the uncertainties of the world. They seek in their partners not just companionship but a bastion of reliability and trustworthiness, a haven where their hearts can rest assured in the steadfastness of their chosen confidants. This deep-seated yearning for security and trust is not born out of fear but rather from a profound understanding of the world's unpredictable nature, mirroring the Enneagram's own journey through myriad spiritual and philosophical landscapes to uncover the core truths of human personality.

The importance of trust for Type 6 women cannot be overstated. It is the golden thread that binds the fabric of their relationships, the silent covenant that transforms an ordinary connection into a sacred alliance. Trust, for them, is not given lightly nor expected to be unearned; it is cultivated with care, nurtured through consistent actions and reassurances, and preserved with the vigilance of a guardian. In the realm of trust, words are weighed for their sincerity, promises are treasured like rare jewels, and betrayals are felt with the intensity of a wound to the soul.

Security, in turn, is the fortress that safeguards the heart of a Type 6 woman. It is constructed from the bricks of mutual understanding, respect, and unwavering support, its foundations anchored in the bedrock of shared values and dreams. In the embrace of a secure relationship, Type 6 women find the courage to face their fears, the strength to weather life's storms, and the freedom to explore the vast landscapes of their inner worlds. Security offers them a mirror in which they can see reflected the best versions of themselves, emboldened by the trust and support of those they love.

However, the path to building trust and security is fraught with challenges. Type 6 women are acutely aware of the fragility of trust, how it can be shattered by a single act of thoughtlessness or betrayal. They understand that security is not a static state but a dynamic process that requires constant attention and effort. Thus, they approach their relationships with a blend of caution and hope, ever vigilant against the shadows of doubt but ever hopeful for the light of genuine connection.

In their partners, Type 6 women seek not just allies but fellow travelers on the journey of life, individuals who understand the sacredness of trust and the value of security. They desire partners who are not intimidated by the complexity of their fears but are willing to stand beside them, offering a steady hand through the darkest nights and celebrating with them under the brightest skies. For a Type 6 woman, the ultimate testament to a relationship's strength lies not in the absence of fear or doubt but in the presence of unwavering support and understanding, the kind that endures through trials and triumphs alike.

As the Enneagram continues to illuminate the diverse landscapes of the human soul, offering insights into the motivations and fears that drive us, the journey of Type 6 women in search of trust and security stands as a testament to the power of relationships to offer refuge, strength, and transformation. In the sanctuary of trusted and secure bonds, Type 6 women find not only shelter from the storms but also the fertile ground in which the seeds of their potential can flourish, nurtured by the love and support of those who understand the profound significance of trust and security in the tapestry of human connections.

Strategies for Fostering Effective Communication and Strengthening Relationships with Partners, Friends, and Family

In the intricate dance of human interaction, where every gesture and word weaves the delicate fabric of our connections, effective communication emerges as the sovereign thread in the tapestry of relationships, especially for Type 6 women. The Enneagram, with its rich history of exploring the depths of human psyche and its motivations, offers a unique lens through which we can understand the communication dynamics crucial for Type 6 women in nurturing their bonds with partners, friends, and family.

Just as the Enneagram's journey from ancient spiritual symbols to a modern tool for self-understanding embodies a confluence of wisdom from diverse traditions, the art of communication for Type 6 women is a blend of openness, authenticity, and empathy, honed through self-awareness and mindful practice. The strategies delineated below serve as guiding stars in the quest for building trust and security through the power of words and beyond.

Cultivating Openness and Vulnerability: At the heart of effective communication lies the courage to be open and vulnerable. For Type 6 women, whose instincts often sway between trust and skepticism, embracing vulnerability can be transformative. By sharing their fears, hopes, and dreams without the armor of pretense, they invite others into their inner world, paving the way for deeper connections. This act of bravery not only diminishes the walls of doubt but also fosters a climate of mutual trust and understanding.

Practicing Active Listening: Active listening is an art that demands the entirety of one's attention, a skill that Type 6 women can master to strengthen their relationships. It involves listening with empathy, acknowledging the emotions behind the words, and responding with thoughtfulness. By practicing active listening, Type 6 women validate the feelings and thoughts of their loved ones, demonstrating their genuine care and interest, which, in turn, enhances the bond of trust and security.

Expressing Appreciation and Affirmation: Words of appreciation and affirmation are like nourishment for relationships. For Type 6 women, expressing gratitude and acknowledging the strengths and efforts of their partners, friends, and family can significantly bolster the sense of security and belonging in the relationship. Such expressions of love and appreciation reinforce the foundation of trust, reminding both parties of their value and importance in each other's lives.

Navigating Conflicts with Compassion and Clarity: Conflicts, when handled with compassion and clarity, can become opportunities for growth in relationships. Type 6 women, with their keen insight into potential issues, can lead the way in resolving conflicts through open communication, seeking to understand before being understood.

Approaching disagreements with a clear intention to find common ground and compromise strengthens relationships, demonstrating that the bond shared is valued above individual differences.

Setting Boundaries with Kindness and Respect: Effective communication also involves the clear articulation of one's needs and boundaries. Type 6 women, in their pursuit of security, benefit greatly from setting and respecting boundaries in their relationships. By communicating their limits with kindness and respect, they not only protect their well-being but also foster a healthy environment where mutual respect and understanding thrive.

In conclusion, as Type 6 women navigate the complexities of their relationships, these strategies of fostering effective communication stand as beacons of light, guiding them towards stronger, more secure bonds. Just as the Enneagram has evolved through centuries, enriching its wisdom from diverse sources, so too can the art of communication evolve within each relationship, building trust and security on the foundations of openness, empathy, and mutual respect. In this endeavor, Type 6 women, armed with their depth of insight and capacity for profound connections, can transform their relationships into havens of trust and security, echoing the timeless journey of the Enneagram towards self-discovery and interpersonal harmony.

Chapter 5:

Meet Your Tribe: Building Support Networks

The Value of Strong Friendships and Social Support for the Type 6 Woman

In the tapestry of life, where each thread represents a connection, a memory, or a moment in time, the value of strong friendships and social support for the Type 6 woman stands out as a vibrant, indelible strand. Much like the Enneagram itself, which traverses through ancient wisdom and philosophical insights to offer a mirror to our innermost selves, the journey of the Type 6 woman is intricately linked to the networks of support that surround her, acting as both a reflection of her inner world and a foundation upon which she builds her sense of security and belonging.

The Enneagram, with its roots deeply embedded in the rich soil of human history and spirituality, teaches us that every personality type navigates the world through a lens shaped by their core desires and fears. For the Type 6 woman, this journey is navigated with a keen sense of vigilance, an innate desire for stability, and a profound longing for trustworthy connections. It is within the realm of strong friendships and robust social networks that Type 6 women find the anchorage they deeply crave, a safe harbor amidst the tempestuous seas of uncertainty and change.

A Sanctuary of Trust: For Type 6 women, friendships are not mere social conveniences; they are sanctuaries of trust. In a world where uncertainty looms large and loyalty often waxes and wanes, the value of a friend who stands unwavering, whose integrity is as steadfast as the ancient pyramids, is immeasurable. These friendships offer a bedrock of reliability, where fears can be shared without judgment, and joys celebrated with genuine enthusiasm.

The Role of Social Support in Navigating Uncertainty: The support network of a Type 6 woman acts as her compass through the fog of life's uncertainties. It is within the collective wisdom of her tribe that she finds guidance, reassurance, and the diverse perspectives needed to navigate her fears and doubts. This social support is not a mere echo chamber but a forum of trusted advisers who provide the strength and insight necessary to face the unknown with courage.

Empowerment through Connection: Strong friendships and social support empower Type 6 women by affirming their worth and capabilities. In the reflection of her friends' eyes, a Type 6 woman sees the best version of herself mirrored back at her, reinforced by the support and faith of those she holds dear. This empowerment is a crucial element in her personal growth journey, providing the confidence to explore new horizons and embrace her full potential.

Building a Network of Mutual Support: The art of building a support network for a Type 6 woman is akin to weaving a tapestry, each thread representing a connection made stronger through mutual support and understanding. It is a reciprocal relationship, where the giving and receiving of support create a tightly knit fabric of communal resilience. In this network, each member is both a contributor and a beneficiary, fostering a sense of collective security and interconnectedness.

In conclusion, as the Enneagram continues to serve as a guide for self-discovery and personal development, the importance of strong friendships and social support for the Type 6 woman cannot be overstated. These relationships are the vessels through which she navigates the complexities of her internal and external worlds, providing the trust, support, and empowerment necessary to traverse the unpredictable landscape of life. As she builds and nurtures her tribe, the Type 6 woman anchors herself in a community of souls who understand her, cherish her, and support her journey towards self-assurance and peace. In the embrace of her support network, she finds not only safety and belonging but also the courage to unfold the wings of her potential, propelled by the collective strength and loyalty of those she calls her tribe.

Tips for Building and Maintaining Strong Relationships with Friends and Colleagues

In the rich narrative of human connection, where the tapestry of our interactions is woven from the threads of myriad encounters and shared experiences, the Enneagram serves as a compass, guiding us through the complexities of our personalities and relationships. For the Type 6 woman, embarking on the journey of building and maintaining strong relationships with friends and colleagues is akin to navigating the ancient trade routes that connected diverse cultures and civilizations, requiring both a keen sense of direction and a profound understanding of the human heart.

Drawing from the wisdom of the Enneagram, which has traversed through the sands of time, capturing the essence of human motivation and fears, this chapter offers a beacon of light to Type 6 women seeking to forge lasting bonds in their personal and professional lives. Here are the strategies, time-tested as the Enneagram itself, designed to strengthen the scaffolding of these essential connections.

Communicate with Authenticity and Clarity: In the realm of relationships, authenticity acts as the cornerstone upon which trust is built. For Type 6 women, who navigate the world with a vigilant eye towards sincerity and reliability, expressing themselves with clarity and honesty is crucial. By sharing their thoughts and feelings openly, they invite a reciprocal exchange of trust, laying the groundwork for deep and meaningful connections.

Cultivate Empathy and Understanding: Empathy is the bridge that connects disparate souls, allowing us to traverse the distance between our own experiences and those of others. For the Type 6 woman, cultivating an empathetic approach to interactions with friends and colleagues is tantamount to deciphering the ancient symbols of the Enneagram, each one a key to understanding the multifaceted nature of human emotions and motivations. By seeking to understand the perspectives and feelings of others, Type 6 women can strengthen the bonds of mutual respect and compassion.

Establish Mutual Support: The journey through life, much like the quest for self-discovery through the Enneagram, is best undertaken with the support of fellow travelers. Type 6 women thrive in environments where mutual support is the norm, where each individual's strengths are recognized and bolstered. By fostering a culture of support in their relationships, Type 6 women not only secure the loyalty and trust of their friends and colleagues but also create a network of allies ready to stand by them through thick and thin.

Practice Consistency and Reliability: Reliability, a trait highly valued by Type 6 women, is the currency of trust in any relationship. By being consistent in their actions and keeping their promises, Type 6 women demonstrate their commitment to the relationship, reinforcing the security and stability that are so crucial to them. This consistency becomes the silent testament to their dedication, earning them the esteem and trust of those around them.

Engage in Shared Activities: Shared experiences are the threads from which the fabric of our relationships is woven. For Type 6 women, engaging in activities that align with their interests and values, alongside friends and colleagues, serves to strengthen their bonds. Whether it's a collaborative project at work or a shared hobby, these experiences foster a sense of camaraderie and belonging, enriching the relationship with memories and accomplishments.

In the grand narrative of the Enneagram, with its roots stretching back to the ancient wisdom of civilizations long gone, the journey of the Type 6 woman in building and maintaining strong relationships reflects the universal quest for connection and understanding. Armed with these strategies, inspired by the enduring teachings of the Enneagram, Type 6 women can navigate the complex waters of human relationships, building bridges of trust and support that stand the test of time. In doing so, they not only enrich their own lives but also contribute to the creation of a more interconnected and compassionate world, echoing the timeless legacy of the Enneagram itself.

Chapter 6

Discovering Your Purpose: Career and Vocation

Identifying Your Strengths and Passions to Find a Meaningful Career

Embarking on the journey to discover one's purpose, especially in the context of career and vocation, is akin to navigating the ancient pathways of self-knowledge that the Enneagram illuminates. For the Type 6 woman, this exploration is both a quest for security and a voyage into the depths of her passions and strengths, guided by the timeless wisdom of this enigmatic system. The Enneagram, with its roots entwined in the rich soil of spiritual and philosophical traditions, offers a compass for this journey, revealing the unique talents and drives that shape the Type 6 woman's professional destiny.

Unveiling the Tapestry of Strengths: The first step in identifying a meaningful career path involves a deep dive into the tapestry of one's inherent strengths. For the Type 6 woman, these strengths often manifest as loyalty, perseverance, and an exceptional ability to foresee challenges and devise strategic solutions. Her analytical mind, combined with a keen sense of responsibility, positions her as a natural problem-solver, capable of navigating complex scenarios with grace and foresight. Recognizing these strengths requires a reflective journey, much like the introspective quest for wisdom that has characterized the Enneagram's history.

Embracing Your Passions: Alongside the discovery of strengths, uncovering one's passions is vital in carving a path that resonates with the heart's deepest desires. For Type 6 women, passions might be found in endeavors that offer security and contribute to the greater good, reflecting their intrinsic motivation to create a stable and just world. Whether drawn to the arts, sciences, social work, or any field in between, it is the passion for making a meaningful impact that fuels their vocational aspirations. Like the seekers of old who delved into the mysteries of the Enneagram, Type 6 women are invited to explore the landscapes of their interests, seeking those pursuits that ignite their enthusiasm and sense of purpose.

Aligning Strengths and Passions with Career Paths: The confluence of strengths and passions points the way toward a fulfilling career. For the Type 6 woman, this might mean roles that allow her to employ her analytical and strategic thinking, perhaps in planning, risk management, or advisory capacities. Alternatively, her loyalty and commitment to social causes may find expression in careers dedicated to community service, healthcare, or education. The key lies in aligning one's natural talents and passions with professional avenues that offer both personal satisfaction and the opportunity to contribute meaningfully to society.

Navigating the Path with Courage and Openness: The journey to discovering a purposeful career is marked by periods of uncertainty and the need for reassurance. For Type 6 women, embracing this journey with courage and an open heart is crucial. It involves trusting in their own abilities, seeking supportive feedback, and remaining open to the unfolding of new opportunities. Much like the explorers of the Enneagram's ancient wisdom, Type 6 women are encouraged to embrace the journey with all its twists and turns, knowing that each step brings them closer to their true calling.

Creating a Legacy of Purpose: In the pursuit of a career that aligns with their strengths and passions, Type 6 women not only secure their own sense of fulfillment but also contribute to the tapestry of the world in a meaningful way. Their legacy is one of purpose, characterized by the impact they make through their chosen vocations. As they navigate their professional paths, guided by the insights of the Enneagram, they weave a narrative of contribution and purpose that echoes through their work and into the lives of those they touch.

In conclusion, as Type 6 women embark on the journey to discover their vocational calling, they are guided by the ancient wisdom of the Enneagram, which serves as a beacon in their quest for purpose. By identifying their strengths and passions, aligning them with meaningful career paths, and navigating the journey with courage and openness, they forge a legacy of impact and fulfillment. In doing so, they not only realize their own potential but also contribute to the greater tapestry of human endeavor, embodying the spirit of growth and discovery that the Enneagram inspires.

Strategies for Overcoming Indecision and Fear of Failure in the Workplace

In the intricate journey of self-discovery and vocational fulfillment, the Enneagram serves as a compass, guiding individuals through the labyrinth of their innermost fears, desires, and strengths. For Type 6 women, this journey is often marked by the challenges of indecision and a pervasive fear of failure, obstacles that can cloud the path to realizing their true potential in the workplace. Yet, just as the ancient wisdom of the Enneagram has illuminated the path to self-knowledge for centuries, so too can it offer strategies to navigate these challenges, empowering Type 6 women to embrace their careers with confidence and purpose.

Embrace a Growth Mindset: At the heart of overcoming the fear of failure is the adoption of a growth mindset, a concept that transcends time, echoing the Enneagram's evolution from ancient symbolism to a tool for modern psychological insight. A growth mindset encourages viewing challenges and setbacks not as insurmountable obstacles but as opportunities for learning and personal development. For Type 6 women, cultivating this mindset means shifting focus from the fear of making mistakes to the potential for growth that each new experience in the workplace offers.

Develop a Decision-Making Framework: Indecision, often fueled by the fear of making the wrong choice, can be paralyzing. To navigate this, Type 6 women can benefit from establishing a structured decision-making framework, reminiscent of the systematic approaches found in the philosophical traditions that underpin the Enneagram. This framework might include setting clear criteria for decisions, seeking advice from trusted mentors, and allowing for a reflective period before making a commitment. Such an approach not only streamlines the decision-making process but also provides a sense of security and control.

Foster a Supportive Network: The value of a supportive network cannot be overstated, echoing the communal philosophies intertwined with the Enneagram's history. For Type 6 women, building relationships with colleagues who provide encouragement, feedback, and reassurance can be a bulwark against the isolating effects of fear and indecision. This network serves as a sounding board for ideas and concerns, offering diverse perspectives that can illuminate the path forward and bolster confidence in decision-making.

Set Incremental Goals: The journey of a thousand miles begins with a single step, a truth as relevant today as it was in the days of the ancient sages who contributed to the Enneagram's lore. For Type 6 women grappling with fear of failure, setting incremental, achievable goals can help build momentum and foster a sense of accomplishment. These small victories not only pave the way for larger successes but also counteract the paralysis of indecision by breaking down daunting tasks into manageable steps.

Practice Mindfulness and Self-Compassion: In the quest to overcome workplace challenges, the practice of mindfulness and self-compassion offers a refuge, much like the spiritual traditions from which the Enneagram draws its roots. For Type 6 women, cultivating mindfulness can enhance present-moment awareness, reducing the anxiety that fuels indecision and fear of failure. Similarly, practicing self-compassion encourages a kind and forgiving attitude towards oneself, fostering resilience in the face of setbacks and challenges.

In conclusion, as Type 6 women embark on their vocational journeys, guided by the ancient wisdom of the Enneagram, they are equipped with strategies to overcome the hurdles of indecision and fear of failure. By embracing a growth mindset, developing a decision-making framework, fostering supportive networks, setting incremental goals, and practicing mindfulness and self-compassion, they can navigate the complexities of the workplace with confidence and grace. In doing so, they not only realize their potential but also contribute their unique strengths and insights to the tapestry of their professional environments, embodying the transformative power of the Enneagram in their pursuit of purpose and fulfillment.

Chapter 7:

Cultivating Inner Strength: Resilience and Self-Compassion

Developing Resilience to Face Challenges and Self-Criticism

In the evolving narrative of the Enneagram, a journey through the ancient corridors of self-understanding and growth, the quest for resilience and self-compassion emerges as a pivotal chapter, especially for the Type 6 woman. The rich tapestry of the Enneagram, woven from the threads of diverse spiritual and philosophical traditions, offers profound insights into the human condition, illuminating the path toward cultivating the inner strength necessary to navigate life's myriad challenges and the often harsh landscape of self-criticism.

The Foundation of Resilience: Resilience, the capacity to rebound from adversity, is akin to the deep roots of an ancient tree, enabling it to withstand the fiercest storms. For the Type 6 woman, developing resilience begins with acknowledging and embracing her inherent strengths—loyalty, perseverance, and an uncanny ability to anticipate and navigate difficulties. This recognition serves as a wellspring of resilience, reminding her that she possesses the inner resources to face life's challenges head-on. Just as the Enneagram's history is marked by a journey of discovery and adaptation, so too is the personal journey of the Type 6 woman, learning to adapt and grow stronger with each challenge encountered.

Transforming Fear into Courage: Central to the Type 6 personality is a vigilance against potential threats, a trait that, while protective, can sometimes spiral into excessive worry or fear. Transforming this fear into courage is a crucial step in developing resilience. This transformation involves a conscious shift in perspective, from seeing challenges as insurmountable obstacles to viewing them as opportunities for growth and learning. Drawing inspiration from the Enneagram's storied evolution, the Type 6 woman can learn to use her analytical skills not as a means to foresee every possible danger but as a tool to strategize and innovate in the face of adversity.

Cultivating Self-Compassion: In the battle against self-criticism, self-compassion emerges as a powerful ally. For the Type 6 woman, who may often find herself entangled in self-doubt and criticism, learning to extend kindness and understanding to herself is transformative. Self-compassion involves recognizing one's own suffering, acknowledging that imperfection is part of the human experience, and treating oneself with the same care and kindness one would offer a dear friend. By integrating self-compassion into her daily life, the Type 6 woman builds a nurturing inner sanctuary, a refuge from the harsh judgments of both the external world and her own inner critic.

Embracing Vulnerability: The journey toward resilience and self-compassion requires the courage to be vulnerable. For Type 6 women, this means allowing themselves to be seen, with all their fears, doubts, and imperfections. Embracing vulnerability is not a sign of weakness but a testament to strength, the strength to acknowledge one's true self and seek connection and support. This step echoes the Enneagram's invitation to explore the depths of our being, to uncover and embrace all aspects of ourselves in the pursuit of growth and self-acceptance.

Building a Supportive Community: The path to resilience is not meant to be walked alone. Just as the Enneagram has evolved through the contributions of countless seekers and scholars, so too does the resilience of the Type 6 woman flourish in the presence of a supportive community. Surrounding herself with individuals who understand, encourage, and challenge her, she finds the strength to persevere through difficulties and the space to practice self-compassion.

as the Type 6 woman embarks on her journey toward cultivating inner strength, the ancient wisdom of the Enneagram serves as both guide and companion. By developing resilience, transforming fear into courage, cultivating self-compassion, embracing vulnerability, and building a supportive community, she not only navigates the challenges of life with grace and tenacity but also moves closer to realizing her fullest potential. This journey, marked by both struggle and triumph, reflects the enduring spirit of the Enneagram itself—a testament to the transformative power of self-discovery and the unyielding resilience of the human spirit.

Techniques for Managing Anxiety and Cultivating Self-Compassion

In the rich and diverse history of the Enneagram, a system that navigates through the complexities of human personality with the grace of ancient wisdom, we find invaluable insights for cultivating inner strength and resilience. For the Type 6 woman, whose journey often involves managing anxiety and fostering a nurturing sense of self-compassion, the teachings of the Enneagram offer a beacon of light. This chapter delves into practical techniques that echo the Enneagram's timeless guidance, enabling Type 6 women to navigate their inner landscapes with confidence and grace.

Mindfulness and Meditation: Drawing from the contemplative practices that have intersected with the Enneagram's philosophical roots, mindfulness and meditation emerge as powerful techniques for managing anxiety. These practices encourage a state of present-moment awareness, allowing Type 6 women to observe their thoughts and feelings without judgment. By anchoring themselves in the here and now, they can create a space of calm amidst the storm of anxieties, learning to respond to life's challenges with equanimity rather than being overwhelmed by them.

Cognitive-Behavioral Techniques: The journey of the Enneagram, much like the path of cognitive-behavioral therapy (CBT), involves uncovering and transforming deep-seated beliefs and patterns. For managing anxiety, Type 6 women can benefit from identifying and challenging their automatic negative thoughts, a common source of their anxiety. By examining the evidence for and against these thoughts, they can begin to reframe their perceptions, reducing the power of unfounded fears and fostering a more balanced and positive outlook.

Journaling for Self-Reflection: The practice of journaling, a method of self-reflection that mirrors the introspective nature of the Enneagram, offers Type 6 women a tool for exploring their inner world. Through writing, they can express their anxieties, hopes, and dreams, engaging in a dialogue with themselves that promotes understanding and compassion. This reflective practice can be particularly therapeutic, helping to diffuse anxiety and cultivate a kinder, more compassionate relationship with oneself.

Building a Support Network: Echoing the communal spirit that underlies the Enneagram's teachings, fostering strong, supportive relationships is key to managing anxiety and developing self-compassion. Type 6 women thrive in environments where they feel understood and supported. By actively seeking out and nurturing relationships with individuals who offer empathy and encouragement, they can create a safety net that bolsters their resilience and mitigates the isolating effects of anxiety.

Practicing Gratitude: The cultivation of gratitude, a practice as timeless as the spiritual traditions from which the Enneagram draws, serves as a potent antidote to anxiety. By focusing on the aspects of their lives for which they are thankful, Type 6 women can shift their attention away from fears and towards appreciation. This shift not only enhances their mood and outlook but also reinforces a sense of connection to the world around them, fostering a deep and abiding sense of well-being.

In conclusion, as Type 6 women embark on their journey toward cultivating inner strength, the ancient wisdom of the Enneagram offers a roadmap for navigating the challenges of anxiety and the cultivation of self-compassion. Through mindfulness and meditation, cognitive-behavioral techniques, journaling for self-reflection, building a supportive network, and practicing gratitude, they can harness their inherent resilience and nurture a compassionate relationship with themselves. In doing so, they honor the Enneagram's legacy as a tool for personal growth and transformation, embodying its principles in their daily lives and finding in themselves a wellspring of strength and serenity.

Chapter 8:

Holistic Well-being: Body and Mind in Balance

The Importance of Mindful Nutrition for the Physical and Emotional Health of the Type 6 Woman

In the vast and intricate landscape of the Enneagram, where each type navigates a unique path toward self-understanding and growth, the concept of holistic well-being emerges as a pivotal theme. For the Type 6 woman, achieving a balance between body and mind is not just a pursuit of health but a foundational aspect of her journey towards stability and security. The ancient wisdom of the Enneagram, with its deep roots in spiritual and philosophical traditions, underscores the interconnectedness of physical and emotional health, offering insights into the critical role of mindful nutrition in nurturing this balance.

Nourishing the Body, Calming the Mind: The principle of mindful nutrition transcends the mere act of eating healthfully; it embodies an intentional and attentive approach to nourishment, recognizing that what we consume has profound effects on both our physical well-being and our emotional state. For the Type 6 woman, whose path often involves managing anxiety and seeking security, mindful nutrition offers a powerful tool for cultivating resilience. By choosing foods that not only nourish the body but also support emotional balance, she can strengthen her foundation of health, thereby enhancing her ability to face life's uncertainties with confidence.

The Connection Between Gut Health and Emotional Well-being: Emerging research underscores the intricate connection between the gut and the brain, revealing how our digestive health can significantly influence our mood and mental state. This gut-brain axis speaks to the wisdom of ancient philosophies integrated within the Enneagram's teachings, which have long recognized the holistic nature of well-being. For the Type 6 woman, prioritizing gut health through mindful nutrition—incorporating probiotics, fiber-rich foods, and a diversity of nutrients—can be a key strategy in managing anxiety and fostering a sense of inner calm.

Mindful Eating Practices: Mindful eating, a practice of being fully present and engaged in the experience of eating, aligns with the Enneagram's emphasis on self-awareness and introspection. For Type 6 women, adopting mindful eating practices can help mitigate stress eating and emotional overeating, common responses to anxiety. By focusing on the senses—the taste, texture, and aroma of food—she can transform eating into a meditative practice, enhancing her connection to her body's signals of hunger and satiety and cultivating gratitude for the nourishment provided.

Strategic Nutrition for Stress Management: Certain foods and nutrients have been shown to have a calming effect on the body and mind, offering strategic support for stress management. For the Type 6 woman, integrating foods rich in omega-3 fatty acids, magnesium, and antioxidants into her diet can support the nervous system and mitigate the physical effects of stress. Additionally, staying hydrated and moderating caffeine and sugar intake can help maintain energy levels and mood stability, empowering her to navigate her day with greater ease and confidence.

Creating a Ritual of Self-Care: Beyond the physical aspects of nutrition, the act of preparing and enjoying meals can serve as a ritual of self-care, a concept deeply embedded in the spiritual traditions that inform the Enneagram. For the Type 6 woman, creating space in her daily routine for these rituals—whether it's brewing a cup of herbal tea, cooking a nourishing meal, or savoring a piece of dark chocolate—can be a powerful affirmation of self-love and a reminder of her commitment to holistic well-being.

as the Type 6 woman journeys through the landscape of the Enneagram towards a deeper understanding of herself and her place in the world, mindful nutrition emerges as a key component of holistic well-being. By embracing the principles of nourishing the body, prioritizing gut health, practicing mindful eating, strategically managing stress through nutrition, and creating rituals of self-care, she cultivates a balance between body and mind that supports her in facing challenges with resilience and grace. This approach not only enhances her physical and emotional health but also aligns with the Enneagram's broader teachings on the interconnectedness of all aspects of our being, guiding her towards a state of harmony and well-being.

The Role of Physical Exercise in Stress Management and Overall Well-being

In the intricate dance of holistic well-being, where the Enneagram guides us through the nuanced pathways of self-discovery and growth, the role of physical exercise emerges as a cornerstone for managing stress and fostering a harmonious balance between body and mind. This chapter delves into the transformative power of physical activity for the Type 6 woman, drawing upon the ancient wisdom of the Enneagram to illuminate the profound impact of exercise on emotional resilience, mental clarity, and physical vitality.

A Pathway to Resilience: Just as the Enneagram has traversed through centuries, evolving alongside the spiritual and philosophical currents of its time, so too does the practice of physical exercise offer a dynamic path to resilience for the Type 6 woman. Engaging in regular physical activity fortifies the body against the physiological impacts of stress, enhancing cardiovascular health, strengthening the immune system, and regulating the body's stress responses. This physical resilience, in turn, supports the Type 6 woman in navigating the uncertainties and anxieties that mark her journey, imbuing her with the strength to face challenges with courage and grace.

Exercise as Meditation in Motion: The ancient traditions from which the Enneagram draws its roots have long celebrated the meditative qualities of physical movement. For the Type 6 woman, exercise can become a form of meditation in motion, a practice that centers the mind and cultivates a state of mindful presence. Whether through yoga, tai chi, running, or dancing, engaging in physical activity with intention and awareness allows her to transcend the chatter of anxiety, connecting her to the here and now. This meditative aspect of exercise serves not only to alleviate stress but also to enhance self-awareness and emotional equilibrium, echoing the introspective journey of the Enneagram.

Strengthening the Mind-Body Connection: The philosophy of the Enneagram teaches us about the interconnectedness of all aspects of our being, a principle that finds vivid expression in the relationship between physical exercise and mental well-being. For the Type 6 woman, incorporating a variety of physical activities into her routine can stimulate neural growth, improve cognitive function, and elevate mood through the release of endorphins. This strengthened mind-body connection fosters a sense of wholeness and well-being, empowering her to approach life's challenges with a balanced and integrated perspective.

Building a Supportive Community Through Exercise: Reflecting the communal spirit that underlies the Enneagram's teachings, the pursuit of physical exercise offers the Type 6 woman an opportunity to connect with others who share her commitment to well-being. Joining a fitness class, hiking group, or sports team not only provides a source of motivation and accountability but also enriches her support network, reinforcing her sense of belonging and security. These social connections, forged through shared activity, contribute to her emotional resilience and enhance the joy of her physical exercise journey.

Customizing Exercise to Foster Joy and Engagement: Recognizing that the journey of each Enneagram type is unique, the Type 6 woman is encouraged to explore and identify the forms of physical activity that resonate most deeply with her interests and needs. By customizing her exercise routine to include activities that she genuinely enjoys, she ensures that her commitment to physical well-being is sustainable and fulfilling. Whether it's the calm of a morning walk, the exhilaration of a dance class, or the focus of martial arts, choosing activities that bring joy and engagement supports her holistic well-being, aligning her physical endeavors with her personal journey of growth and discovery.

Chapter 9:

The Enneagram and Spirituality: Deepening Your Connection

Exploring Various Spiritual Practices That Resonate with Type 6 Women

Within the rich landscape of the Enneagram's history—a tapestry interwoven with threads of ancient wisdom, philosophical depth, and spiritual insight—lies the key to unlocking a myriad of spiritual practices tailored to the unique journey of the Type 6 woman. As seekers of security and advocates of loyalty, Type 6 women are naturally inclined towards spiritual practices that foster a sense of inner stability and connectedness, grounding them in the face of life's uncertainties. This chapter ventures into the exploration of spiritual practices that resonate deeply with the essence of the Type 6 woman, aiding her in the quest for deeper connection and spiritual fulfillment.

Meditation and Mindfulness: Rooted in the ancient traditions that also inform the Enneagram, meditation and mindfulness offer Type 6 women a sanctuary of calm amidst the storm of their worries and anxieties. Practices such as guided meditation, mindfulness-based stress reduction (MBSR), and loving-kindness meditation (Metta) provide a framework for cultivating presence, compassion, and self-acceptance. These practices not only soothe the anxious mind but also deepen the spiritual connection by fostering a moment-to-moment awareness of the divine presence in all aspects of life.

Contemplative Prayer: Drawing on the mystical traditions that have paralleled the Enneagram's development, contemplative prayer is a practice that invites Type 6 women into a deep, silent communion with the divine. This form of prayer, which emphasizes inner stillness and the letting go of thoughts, aligns with the Type 6's longing for guidance and support from a higher power. By surrendering their fears and uncertainties in contemplative prayer, Type 6 women open themselves to receiving divine wisdom and comfort, reinforcing their trust in the spiritual journey.

Journaling as a Spiritual Practice: The reflective nature of journaling makes it a powerful spiritual tool for Type 6 women, allowing them to articulate their fears, hopes, and spiritual insights. Through the written word, they can explore the depths of their inner landscape, identify patterns of thought and behavior that hinder their spiritual growth, and document moments of grace and revelation. This practice serves as both a mirror and a map, reflecting their spiritual progress and guiding them towards greater self-understanding and acceptance.

Nature-Based Spirituality: For Type 6 women, who often seek stability and reassurance, connecting with the natural world can be a profoundly spiritual experience. Practices such as forest bathing, gardening, or simply spending time in contemplative appreciation of nature's beauty and resilience, can remind them of the interconnectedness of all life and the enduring presence of the divine in the natural world. This connection to nature nurtures their soul, offering a grounding and rejuvenating spiritual practice that counters the chaos of everyday life.

Community and Fellowship: Recognizing the importance of supportive relationships in the Type 6's journey, engaging in community-based spiritual practices can be particularly fulfilling. Whether it's participating in group worship, spiritual study groups, or community service projects, these collective experiences strengthen the Type 6 woman's sense of belonging and connectedness to something greater than herself. Within these communities, she finds not only a source of spiritual nourishment but also the opportunity to offer her gifts of loyalty and service to others.

Exploring Various Spiritual Practices That Resonate with Type 6 Women

The Enneagram, with its rich tapestry woven from the ancient threads of spiritual and philosophical traditions, serves as a profound guide for personal and spiritual development. Particularly for Type 6 women, whose journey is often marked by a search for security and a deep desire for meaningful connections, the Enneagram offers a beacon of insight, illuminating the path toward a deeper spiritual engagement. This chapter explores a spectrum of spiritual practices that resonate with the essence of Type 6 women, facilitating a journey of exploration, connection, and transformation.

Sacred Reading and Reflection: The practice of sacred reading, or lectio divina, a method steeped in the traditions that inform the Enneagram, offers Type 6 women a reflective and meditative approach to spirituality. This practice involves reading spiritual texts slowly and contemplatively, allowing the words to resonate deeply. Through this process, Type 6 women can find guidance, comfort, and a deeper understanding of their spiritual journey, turning their quest for security into a profound exploration of faith.

Guided Imagery and Visualization: Drawing on the imaginative and introspective qualities that often characterize Type 6 individuals, guided imagery and visualization exercises can serve as powerful tools for spiritual exploration. These practices involve visualizing sacred images or scenes, facilitating a deep emotional and spiritual connection. For Type 6 women, this can be a pathway to experiencing a sense of divine presence, easing their fears and nurturing their faith in a supportive and protective universe.

Spiritual Direction: The journey of a Type 6 woman can greatly benefit from the guidance of a spiritual director, a role deeply rooted in the spiritual traditions that parallel the history of the Enneagram. A spiritual director can offer personalized guidance, helping to navigate the complexities of spiritual questions and concerns. This relationship provides a safe space for Type 6 women to explore their doubts, fears, and aspirations, fostering a journey of spiritual discovery grounded in trust and mutual respect.

Group Support and Spiritual Communities: Reflecting the communal aspects of the Enneagram's teachings, participation in spiritual communities or support groups can be particularly enriching for Type 6 women. These settings offer a sense of belonging and a shared space for spiritual exploration. Whether through workshops, retreats, or regular meetings, engaging with a community of like-minded individuals can provide the external assurance and internal peace Type 6 women seek, reinforcing their spiritual path with the strength of collective wisdom and support.

Mindful Movement Practices: Incorporating the body in spiritual practice, through yoga, tai chi, or other mindful movement, aligns with the Enneagram's holistic view of personal development. For Type 6 women, these practices offer a way to ground themselves in the present moment, reducing anxiety and cultivating a sense of inner calm. The physical engagement combined with spiritual intention can enhance their sense of connectedness to their body, mind, and spirit, fostering a balanced approach to their spiritual journey.

In weaving together these various strands of spiritual practice, Type 6 women embark on a multifaceted journey of growth and discovery. The Enneagram, serving as both map and compass, guides them through the landscapes of their inner world, towards a deeper understanding and connection with the divine. By engaging with these practices, Type 6 women can transform their search for security into a profound exploration of spirituality, finding solace in the knowledge that they are guided, protected, and deeply connected to a larger, spiritual reality. This journey, enriched by the ancient wisdom of the Enneagram, invites them into a deeper engagement with the mysteries of their soul and the universe, fostering a journey of faith, resilience, and spiritual awakening.

Chapter 10:

Your Wings: Unfolding Your Complexity

Description of the Wings (Type 6w5 and Type 6w7) and Their Influence on the Personality, Strengths, and Challenges of the Type 6 Woman

In the journey through the Enneagram, a system as rich in history as it is in depth, we discover that each personality type is influenced by its neighboring types, known as "wings". These wings add layers of complexity, strengths, and challenges to the core type, much like the intricate brushstrokes that define a masterpiece. For the Type 6 woman, the influence of her wings, Types 5 and 7, offers a fascinating exploration into the nuances of her personality, providing insights into her inner world and guiding her path of personal growth. This chapter delves into the realms of Type 6w5 and Type 6w7, shedding light on how these wings influence the Type 6 woman's personality, strengths, and challenges.

Type 6w5: The Defender

The Type 6w5, known as the Defender, combines the loyalty and commitment of Type 6 with the intellectual curiosity and independence of Type 5. This blend results in a personality that is both perceptive and analytical, marked by a deep desire to understand the world's complexities. Type 6w5 women are often introspective, seeking knowledge to build security and make sense of their surroundings. They are cautious and thoughtful, with a keen eye for detail and a profound ability to strategize.

Strengths: The Type 6w5 woman excels in environments that require analytical thinking and problem-solving. Her ability to foresee potential issues and meticulously plan for them makes her an invaluable asset in any team. She is driven by a quest for knowledge, which fuels her continuous learning and adaptability. Her blend of loyalty and independence means she is a reliable yet self-sufficient individual, capable of profound insight and innovation.

Challenges: The introspective nature of the Type 6w5 can sometimes lead to isolation, as she may retreat into her inner world, especially when feeling anxious or overwhelmed. Her analytical mind can become a double-edged sword, leading to overthinking and an inability to trust easily, both in personal and professional contexts. Finding a balance between her need for independence and her desire for security can be a significant challenge.

Type 6w7: The Buddy

Type 6w7, known as the Buddy, brings together the security-seeking nature of Type 6 with the enthusiasm and optimism of Type 7. This combination creates a personality that is both loyal and adventurous, capable of facing the world with a sense of preparedness and a desire for experiences. Type 6w7 women are engaging and personable, with a knack for easing tension and bringing a light-heartedness to their environments. They seek stability but are also drawn to the excitement of new opportunities and adventures.

Strengths: The Type 6w7 woman's blend of pragmatism and optimism allows her to navigate challenges with resilience and a positive outlook. She is adaptable, capable of finding joy even in difficult circumstances, and her infectious enthusiasm can uplift and inspire those around her. Her loyalty, coupled with her sociable nature, makes her a cherished friend and colleague, always ready to support and encourage.

Challenges: The desire for security inherent in Type 6 can sometimes clash with the Type 7 wing's longing for freedom and variety, leading to internal conflict. This can manifest as difficulty in making decisions, particularly when it comes to committing to long-term plans or goals. Additionally, the Type 6w7's tendency to seek distractions and experiences can be a way of avoiding deeper anxieties, which, if left unaddressed, can hinder personal growth and fulfillment.

the wings of the Type 6 woman, whether leaning towards the contemplative depth of the 5 or the adventurous spirit of the 7, enrich her personality with a dynamic interplay of qualities. Understanding and embracing the influence of these wings allows the Type 6 woman to navigate her fears and challenges with increased awareness and strength. As she unfolds the complexity of her wings, she gains access to a broader spectrum of strategies for growth, resilience, and fulfillment, guided by the timeless wisdom of the Enneagram. This journey of discovery, underpinned by the ancient teachings of the Enneagram, invites her to embrace the fullness of her being, weaving together the threads of her personality into a cohesive and vibrant tapestry of self.

Chapter 11:

Integration and Disintegration: On the Path of Evolution

Understanding the Integration Process Towards Type 9 and Disintegration Towards Type 3 of the Type 6 Woman

In the intricate and transformative journey of self-evolution that the Enneagram maps out, the concepts of integration and disintegration represent pivotal movements within the psyche of each personality type. For the Type 6 woman, this journey involves the dynamic interplay between moving towards Type 9 in times of growth and towards Type 3 during periods of stress. This chapter delves into the nuances of these processes, offering insights into how they manifest in the life of a Type 6 woman, thereby illuminating a path of evolution that is both challenging and profoundly rewarding.

Integration Towards Type 9: The Path of Peace and Reassurance

As Type 6 women embark on their journey of personal growth and integration, they naturally gravitate towards the healthier aspects of Type 9 – the Peacemaker. This movement signifies a profound shift from a state of constant vigilance and anxiety towards one of inner peace, stability, and trust in the process of life. In this state of integration, Type 6 women begin to embody the serene confidence and acceptance characteristic of Type 9, allowing them to navigate their fears with a grounded sense of calm and a deepened trust in themselves and others.

Characteristics of Integration:

Calmness in Uncertainty: Embracing the Type 9's ability to remain serene amidst chaos, Type 6 women learn to maintain their composure, viewing uncertainties as part of the natural flow of life rather than threats to be incessantly guarded against.

Increased Trust: The journey towards Type 9 fosters a nurturing environment where trust flourishes – trust in the self, in others, and in the unfolding of life's events, diminishing the pervasive doubt that often clouds their judgment.

Adaptive Conflict Resolution: Mirroring Type 9's aversion to conflict but also their ability to mediate, Type 6 women develop a more harmonious approach to resolving disputes, seeking solutions that honor the perspectives and needs of all involved.

Disintegration Towards Type 3: The Path of Stress and Achievement

In contrast, during periods of stress or uncertainty, Type 6 women may find themselves veering towards the less healthy characteristics of Type 3 – the Achiever. This movement reflects a shift from seeking security and support to an adaptive but ultimately unfulfilling pursuit of success, recognition, and productivity as means to counteract underlying anxieties.

Characteristics of Disintegration:

Overemphasis on Efficiency: Under stress, Type 6 women may adopt the Type 3's focus on efficiency and accomplishment, pushing themselves to achieve and perform, often at the expense of their well-being and authentic desires.

Image Consciousness: The disintegration towards Type 3 can manifest in a preoccupation with image and status, where Type 6 women might find themselves overly concerned with how others perceive their success and reliability.

Detachment from Feelings: Mimicking the unhealthy Type 3's tendency to detach from emotions in favor of action, Type 6 women may suppress their feelings, viewing them as obstacles to achievement and stability.

Navigating the Path of Evolution

The journey of integration and disintegration for the Type 6 woman is not a linear path but a cyclical process of evolution, marked by moments of profound growth as well as challenges. By understanding the influences of their movements towards Type 9 and Type 3, Type 6 women can navigate their path with greater awareness, embracing the lessons of each phase. This awareness fosters resilience, enabling them to lean into the growth offered by integration towards Type 9, while also recognizing and addressing the signs of stress that lead towards disintegration to Type 3.

In embracing the dynamic interplay between these movements, the Type 6 woman embarks on a journey of self-discovery that is deeply transformative, guided by the ancient wisdom of the Enneagram. This journey invites her to explore the depths of her complexity, unfolding her potential in a way that is authentic, balanced, and aligned with her true essence. Through this process of continuous evolution, she finds not only peace and stability but also a profound connection to her inner strength and resilience, illuminating the path towards holistic well-being and spiritual fulfillment.

Chapter 12:

Workbook

Did you love *The Woman of Enneagram 6: Love, Marriage, Success Edition*? Then you should read *The woman of Enneagram 5: Love marriage success edition*[1] by Maria Rondon!

[2]

Enneagram Type 5 Woman: Embracing Insight and Growth

Unlock the profound insights of the Enneagram tailored specifically for Type 5 women. This transformative book unveils the intricate layers of the Investigator personality, providing invaluable guidance on core motivations, inherent strengths, and avenues for personal development.

As an Enneagram Type 5 woman, your pursuit of knowledge, understanding, and independence shapes your journey through life. While these qualities are commendable, they can also lead to isolation, detachment, and a fear of being overwhelmed by the demands of the

---

1. https://books2read.com/u/bQGZ2P

2. https://books2read.com/u/bQGZ2P

world. This book empowers you to embrace your authentic self while transcending limiting patterns.

Through engaging exercises and real-world illustrations, you'll delve into how the Enneagram influences your relationships (Enneagram in Love, Enneagram in Marriage), career choices, and personal growth trajectory. Deepen your comprehension of your inner drives, cultivate a balanced perspective, and nurture self-compassion and equilibrium.

Also by Maria Rondon

Alzheimer
Alzheimer Guia para cuidadores

Enneagram For Women
The woman of Enneagram 1: Love Marriage Success Edition
The woman of enneagram 2
The woman of Enneagram 3: Love marriage success edition
The Woman of Enneagram 4: Love, Marriage, Success Edition
The woman of Enneagram 5: Love marriage success edition
The Woman of Enneagram 6: Love, Marriage, Success Edition
The woman of Enneagram 7: Love marriage success edition
The woman of Enneagram 8: Love marriage success edition
The woman of Enneagram 9: Love marriage success edition

LOA
El secreto para atraer tu alma gemela